I AM CHRISTIAN, but what is THE TRINITY?

Written by **MICHELLE MORGAN SPADY**

Illustrated by **MORGYN CHILDS**

For my friend,

Linda Washington-Robinson,

you were my spark of sunshine,

my muse for inspiration,

my encourager and supporter,

and above all, a dear FRIEND.

Thank you, and I love you!

Foreword

Faith is a journey of seeking understanding. It is a journey that requires help and guidance from others. Thank God that God places people in our lives to assist with this quest for understanding. In fact, God will send individuals who are gifted in teaching us more about who God is. Michelle Spady is one of those gifted by God and knowledgeable about God to help us understand more of God.

Michelle has given us a profound, yet simplistic understanding about the things of God. This book provides us with a helpful way for parents to not only learn, but also to teach their children about the doctrines of the Trinity. As a child, learning about the Trinity was one of the most exciting lessons I learned. The study would leave me in awe and wanting to know more. If I had had this book as a child, it would have satisfied my thirst for more. Now, serving as a pastor, this must be included in our core curriculum for Sunday school and our Youth & Teens Ministry.

Children who read this book will not only learn how to be Christians, but they will also be equipped with more knowledge about God the Father, God the Son, and God the Holy Spirit. At times, The Holy Spirit was often discussed and taught in a unilateral way, or not mentioned at all. Michelle embraces the truths about the Holy Spirit based on Biblical foundations and not denominational affiliation.

A pragmatic approach to understanding Christianity and the Trinity in this book is matched with incredible illustrations. The artwork lends strength to the overall message and captures the essence of "I AM A CHRISTIAN, BUT WHAT IS THE TRINITY?" What a great read. I look forward to reading this with my 3-year-old.

Rev. Dr. Robert F. Cheeks, Jr.
Senior Pastor
Shiloh Baptist Church
McLean, VA

Letter to Parents

Dear Parents, Teachers, and Caregivers:

I hope that you will find this book helpful as you introduce your children and students to the Christian doctrine of the Holy Trinity. As you know, the Holy Trinity is a very complex subject to talk about and explain to children; even adults have problems trying to sort it all out!

This book intends to serve as a guide as you begin to teach about the foundational principles of Christianity. The content of the book was designed for a diverse age group and also to introduce BIG words and BIG concepts, allowing for limitless discussions about how BIG our God is.

This book can be read by students individually (student-centered) or accompanied by an adult (teacher-centered). We should never underestimate children's abilities to learn new things, especially about their faith!

The Scriptures cited are just the basics of support that can be found in the Holy Bible to further substantiate and reference the facts in this book.

Also included is the Nicene Creed, the true orthodoxy of the Christian faith, which may prove invaluable in your teachings as your students progress in their studies, and mature on their Christian journey.

Enjoy learning, studying, and teaching! Above all, encourage students to practice the biblical truths so that they may become the people God made them to be.

Michelle Morgan Spady
Author

"Hi, Mom!"

"Hi, Terrance, what's up?"

"Mom, I was just thinking about what our Sunday School Teacher was talking about on Sunday."

"What was that?"

"Well, she talked a lot about the Trinity. I'm not sure I really understood everything. What IS the Trinity, Mom?

"Let's set up a ZOOM session with Pastor CeeCee. She'll explain it to you."

"Okay, let's do it!"

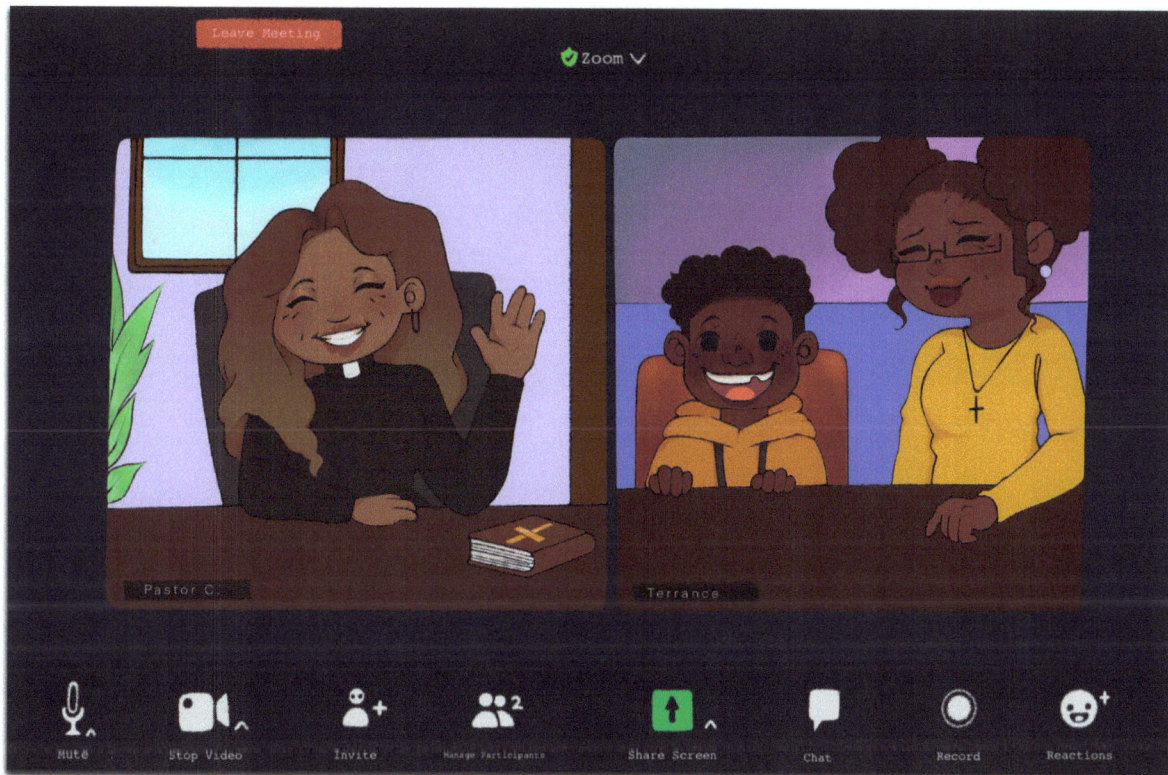

"Hey, Pastor CeeCee, I'm Terrance. What is the Trinity?"

"Hi, Terrance, I know you! Before we talk about the Trinity, let's talk about who we are as Christians, okay?

"Okay!"

"And after that, we'll talk about God and the Holy Trinity. Ready?"

"I'm ready, Pastor CeeCee!"

"Okay, so Christians are people who believe that
Jesus Christ is the Son of God.
They also believe that God sent Jesus to earth to
save us from our sins.
A Christian also trusts and follows the teachings of Jesus Christ.
Jesus taught many things that Christians should do.

Some things Christians do are:

Pray.

Read and study their bibles.

Go to church.

Serve their communities.

Follow God's Word.

LOVE one another!

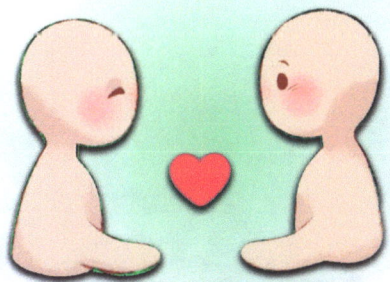

Jesus said, "By this everyone will know that you are my disciples, if you love one another. "(NIV)

John 13:35

JOY

Kindness

Peace

Patience

Faithfulness

Goodness

If a Christian wants to please
the Lord, they should
live a life of:

Joy
Peace
Patience
Kindness
Goodness
Faithfulness
Gentleness
Self-Control

Self Control

Gentleness

God calls these things 'Fruit of the Spirit'.
Galatians 5:22-23

Christians believe in:

God the Father

God the Son

AND

The Holy Spirit

Now, let's talk
about God

We are Christians, so
we believe that:

✝ There is only ONE God.

✝ God has always been around. He has always pre-existed.

✝ God made the heavens and the earth.

✝ God made the birds, the bees, the trees, and you and me!

✝ God is happy and wants us to be happy like Him.

✝ God is compassionate and loving. He wants us to love
others as He loves us.

**Deuteronomy 4:35-36, 6:4 *Genesis 1:1-27 1Timothy 1:17
*Isaiah 45:21-22 *46:5-11 * Matthew 19:26 *1Corinthinans 8:4**

And...God is everywhere. He is **Omnipresent**.

God knows everything. He is **Omniscient**.

God is powerful. He is **Omnipotent**.

God is holy.

God does not change. He is **Immutable**.

God's greatness is beyond language!

Hebrews 13:8 *Psalm 90:2 *Psalm 139-6
***Isaiah 46:10 *Jeremiah 23:23-24*Acts 17:28**

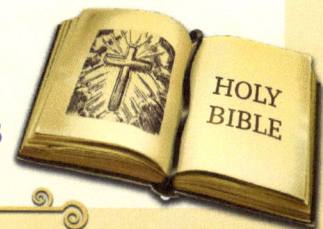

What do we know
about God?

There are some things about God that we just can't explain.

✝ Humans can only understand a certain amount of things about our BIG God.

✝ God is ONE God in three persons: the Father, the Son, and the Holy Spirit. The three persons are each different from one another.

✝ They are distinct, but each one is God.

✝ They have the same characteristics, yet they each work in our lives in special ways.

✝ They think. They act. They feel. They lead. They guide. They comfort. They heal. They work in harmony. They LOVE each other.

✝ This is called the Trinity. ONE GOD is three persons. A 'Mystery Miracle' of God.

What do we understand about the

Holy Trinity?

✝ We understand that the word 'trinity' means three.

✝ We understand that the Holy Trinity is made up of God as three persons.

✝ We understand that God is the Father, and the Father is part of the Trinity.

✝ We understand that God has a Son who became a human like us: Jesus. The Son is the second part of the Trinity.

✝ We understand that God is the Holy Spirit and is the third part of the Trinity.

✝ We understand that some things cannot be explained, but as Christians, we believe and have faith.

Who is the
Father?

God is the Father and Creator of the whole universe!

✝ God left his Word and commandments for us to live by written in a BIG book called The Bible.

✝ The Bible has 66 books with two sections. One section is the Old Testament, and the other section is the New Testament.

✝ There are 39 books in the Old Testament and 27 books in the New Testament. 39 books + 27 books=66 books. That's the whole Bible!

✝ God used many people to write the Bible, like Moses in Exodus.

✝ There were about 35 to 40 named authors of the Bible. Some books we don't know who wrote, like Judges.

✝ Christians and many others use the Bible as instructions to live by, being kind and loving others as God loves us.

1Corinthians 8:6*2Timothy 3:16 *Ephesians 4:6*Exodus 3:13-15 *Judges 13:17-18 *Psalms 8:1; 75:1*Exodus 20:7*Matt 6:9

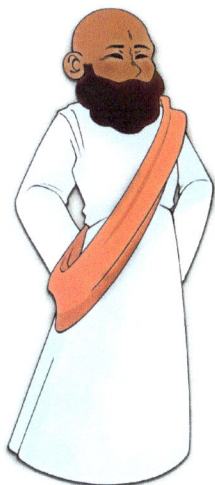

Who is the
Son?

Jesus is the Son of God, he was sent to earth to teach people the truth.

✟ God the Father sent His Son from Heaven to earth, to be born as a baby to two special parents. It was a 'Virgin birth'. This means that God did all the work!

✟ God sent His Son to earth to live with us, teach us, and die on a cross for our sins.

✟ The Son's name is Jesus.

✟ Jesus' special Mom was Mary. His special Dad was Joseph.

✟ Jesus is God. He never sinned, but we did.

✟ Jesus is the eternal Son of God, the second part of the Trinity.

**John 1:1*John 1:14-18*John 3:16*John 8:5-8
*Hebrews 1:3*John 10:30**

14

Jesus died

on the cross for our sins, but that is not how the story ends...

✝ Jesus died on the cross.

✝ Jesus was buried.

✝ Three days later, Jesus came back to life!

✝ This is another 'Mystery Miracle' of God.

✝ Jesus is alive. He is our Savior. You can get to know Him so that one day you can meet Him and God, our Father, face-to-face.

2Corinthians 5:15*Acts 5:30*1Thessalonians 4:14
1Corinthians 15:4*Acts 2:24

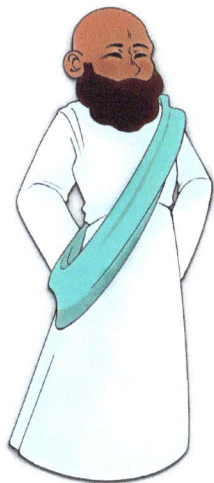

Who is the
Holy Spirit?

The Holy Spirit is with us on earth.

✝ The Holy Spirit is the third person of God.

✝ After Jesus died on the cross, He went back to Heaven to live with God, our Father.

✝ God the Father, and God the Son, sent the Holy Spirit to be with us forever and ever.

✝ The Holy Spirit lives in our hearts and teaches us many neat things like how to pray and understand Jesus and God.

John 14:26*Romans *8:27*1Corinthians 2:10-13
*Ephesians 4:30*Acts 8:29*14:16-17*Matthew 12:31-32

"Well, Terrance," said Pastor CeeCee, "did you learn anything more about the Holy Trinity?"

"Yes, Pastor CeeCee. Thank you so much!" Terrance beamed with pride. "I can't wait for Sunday School to share with my class how much I know about the Holy Trinity."

"Do you have any questions? That was quite a bit of information, Terrance."

"No, that's it for now. Thanks so much. I'll see you on Sunday!"

Closing his laptop, Terrance stood up and hugged his Mother's knees.
"Thank you, Mom, for helping me learn so much about our God, His Son, Jesus Christ, and the Holy Spirit! I love you, Mom!
"You're welcome, son. Love you too!" she said
as she hugged him back.

Story Guide and Activities

Character Background to
Understand the Story

Why do they all look alike? That's because God is three persons in one!

The Father is wearing the white robe to represent Heaven, and the gold sash to represent Deity, Sovereignty, Creator of All Things.

The Son is wearing the white robe to represent Heaven and divinity, and the brown sash to represent His humanity, His dual nature of fully divine and fully human.

The Holy Spirit is wearing the white robe to represent Heaven and divinity, and the green sash to represent new life.

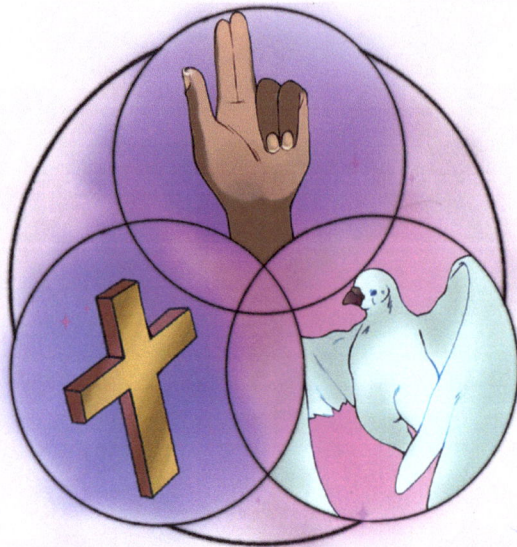

The Trinity Symbol

The Trinity symbol represents, unity and love between the three persons.

The fingers pointed upward represent the Father.

The cross represents the Son.

The dove represents the Holy Spirit.

The big circle surrounding the three reminds us that God is ONE and God is love, and represents the love that flows between the three.

"And so, we know and rely on the love God has for us. God is love. Whoever lives in love lives in God, and God in them.
1John 4:16 (NIV)

Activity

Can you find these Scriptures in the Bible and share them with a friend?

From the Old Testament

Psalm 45:6-7

Isaiah 44:6

Daniel 7:13-14

Isaiah 48:16

Isaiah 63:8-11, 15-17

From the New Testament

Matthew 28:19

John 14:16-17

John 15:26

1Corinthians 12:4-5

2Corinthians 13:14

Ephesians 1:1-14

BIG Word Vocabulary

How many of these BIG words do you remember from the story? Can you find the words again and write the definition?

✝ Christian
✝ Immutable
✝ New Testament
✝ Omnipresent
✝ Omnipotent
✝ Omniscient
✝ Old Testament
✝ Scriptures
✝ Symbol
✝ Trinity

The Nicene Creed

I believe in one God,
the Father almighty,
maker of heaven and earth,
of all things visible and invisible.
I believe in one Lord Jesus Christ,
the Only Begotten Son of God,
born of the Father before all ages.
God from God, Light from Light,
true God from true God,
begotten, not made, consubstantial with the Father;
through him, all things were made.
For us men and for our salvation
he came down from heaven,
and by the Holy Spirit was incarnate of the Virgin Mary,
and became man.
For our sake, he was crucified under Pontius Pilate,
he suffered death and was buried,
and rose again on the third day
in accordance with the Scriptures.
He ascended into heaven
and is seated at the right hand of the Father.
He will come again in glory
to judge the living and the dead
and his kingdom will have no end.
I believe in the Holy Spirit, the Lord, the giver of life,
who proceeds from the Father [and the Son],
who with the Father and the Son is adored and glorified,
who has spoken through the prophets.
I believe in one, holy, catholic and apostolic Church.
I confess one Baptism for the forgiveness of sins,
and I look forward to the resurrection of the dead
and the life of the world to come. Amen.

www.ingramcontent.com/pod-product-compliance
Lightning Source LLC
Chambersburg PA
CBHW042110040426
42448CB00002B/204

9 781736 446805